Alina Stetsyuk

How Football Made Us a Team

A Social Emotional Learning and Regulation Book for Kids Ages 5-7 About Friendship | A Tale of Friendship, Respect and Working Together

TINY THORNS, BIG HEARTS

SERIES "Tiny Thorns, Big Hearts"

Copyright Message:

© 2025 ALINA STETSYUK

All rights reserved. No part of this publication may be reproduced, distributed, or transmitted in any form or by any means, including photocopying, recording, or other electronic or mechanical methods, without the prior written permission of the publisher, except in the case of brief quotations embodied in critical reviews and specific other noncommercial uses permitted by copyright law.

For permissions requests or inquiries, contact alinastetsyukwriter@gmail.com

Dear Readers,

Welcome to Tiny Thorns, Big Hearts - a collection of heartwarming tales about kindness, courage, and the power of understanding.

Through these stories, you'll meet characters who learn to respect boundaries, discover the beauty of friendship, and embrace the strength that comes from both self-love and compassion for others. Each tale is a gentle reminder that even the smallest gestures of kindness can make the biggest difference.

The tiny thorns in these stories represent the little challenges we all face — moments of misunderstanding, impatience, or uncertainty. But big hearts always find a way to grow, to listen, and to connect. Whether it's a young cactus learning about personal space, a lost season rediscovering its purpose, or an unexpected friendship forming in the most unusual way, each story carries a lesson to take with you.

So, dear reader, settle in, turn the page, and let these tales remind you that every heart has room to grow - no matter how small or prickly it may seem.

Warm regards,
Alina Stetsyuk

Far, far away, in a glowing stardust valley where moonbeams made the grass shimmer and the night sky bloomed with a million sparkling lights, there was a magical little town called Shinelightia.

That's where five twinkly little star-kids lived - friends named Sparky, Lum, Blinky, Shyna, and Twig. Each one was full of sparkle, energy, and big-sky dreams.

One warm evening, the friends gathered on the glowing field for their favorite game: football under the stars!

But something felt… off.

"I'm the fastest!" shouted Sparky, puffing up his chest. "No one can outrun me!"

"Well, I'm the smartest!" Shyna chimed in, flipping her hair. "I can predict every move before it happens!"

"That's not fair!" grumbled Lum. "I'm the best kicker here - but no one ever listens to me!"

Soon, everyone was shouting over each other. The field buzzed with noise and fussing.

Then came Coach Glow, the oldest and wisest star of them all. His beams were silver and soft, and when he stepped onto the field, even the grass seemed to hush.

"What's all this ruckus, my shining friends?" he asked, folding his arms gently. "Did someone forget why we play? Who told you this game was about proving who's better?"

"But I really am the fastest!" Sparky piped up. "And I really am the smartest!" Shyna insisted.

Coach Glow smiled, his eyes shining.

"Listen, little starlights. We've got three teams, each with different talents - like morning dew and midnight mist, both beautiful but not the same. You can't compare them.

And remember - football isn't about 'me,' it's about us. You win and stumble together, as a team."

The players fell quiet. One by one, they looked around... and suddenly, the kids didn't see rivals anymore.

They saw teammates. Friends. Fellow dreamers who loved the game just like they did.

"I think we can win," Lum said softly, "if we actually listen to each other."

"And support one another," added Shyna, giving Lum a nod.

And have FUN!" Sparky shouted, kicking the ball up toward the stars.

From that night on, the glowing field of Shinelightia shimmered not just with moonlight, but with laughter, high-fives, and the magic of true teamwork.

Because every player learned one bright truth:

When you shine together, your sparkle gets even brighter.

Afterword

This tale reminds remind us that we all shine in our own way - but when we listen, share, and lift each other up, our light becomes even brighter.

In teams, classrooms, and friendships, it's easy to feel like we have to prove ourselves - to be the fastest, the smartest, or the best. But just like Coach Glow taught the friends, the real magic happens when we stop competing and start connecting.

Whether it's passing the ball, cheering for someone else's success, or simply listening with care - every small act of teamwork adds to something bigger than us: trust, joy, and a sparkle that never fades.

Parent & Child Activity: Shine Brighter Together!

Play, Talk, and Sparkle With Your Little Star

1. **My Team Superpower.** Ask: "What's one way you help a team shine?" Ideas: "I listen," "I help when someone falls," "I make people laugh." Swap roles and answer for yourself too!

2. **The Listening Game.** Take turns giving fun instructions - like "Clap twice and whisper 'Shine!'" But here's the catch: you must wait and listen to the full sentence before acting. Talk about how listening helps us work (and play!) better together.

3. **Shine Jar.** Create a jar and decorate it with stars. Each time your child shows teamwork or empathy (like helping a sibling, waiting their turn, or cheering up a friend), drop in a glow star or shiny coin. When it's full, celebrate with a "Star Power Party" - dance, draw, or read under a cozy blanket.

4. **Teamwork Check-in.** At the end of the day, ask:
   - "Did anyone help you shine today?"
   - "Did you help someone else feel bright?"
   Celebrate both moments with a high-five or hug.

5. **Sparkle Statements.** Say: "We all shine differently!" Then fill in the blank together:
   - "My sparkle is _____." (e.g., kindness, courage, patience, creativity). Post it on the fridge as a daily reminder.

www.ingramcontent.com/pod-product-compliance
Lightning Source LLC
LaVergne TN
LVHW021946060526
838200LV00042B/1937